LOTS OF
Feelings

SHELLEY ROTNER

McGraw Hill **Wright Group**

The **McGraw-Hill** Companies

To my editor, Jean Reynolds, who always makes me feel valued as an author and photographer.

www.WrightGroup.com

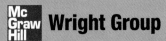 **Wright Group**

Send all inquiries to:
Wright Group/McGraw-Hill
P.O. Box 812960
Chicago, IL 60681

ISBN 978-0-07-658175-7
MHID 0-07-658175-6

4 5 6 7 8 9 DRN 16 15 14 13 12 11

We have lots of feelings.

3

Sometimes
we feel
happy,

4

sometimes
sad.

5

Sometimes we're **grumpy,**

other
times
excited.

7

At times
we feel
shy

8

and
other
times
proud.

9

We
feel
angry
at
times

and **loving**
other times.

Some things **surprise** us.

Other
things
frighten
us.

There are times
we feel
thoughtful

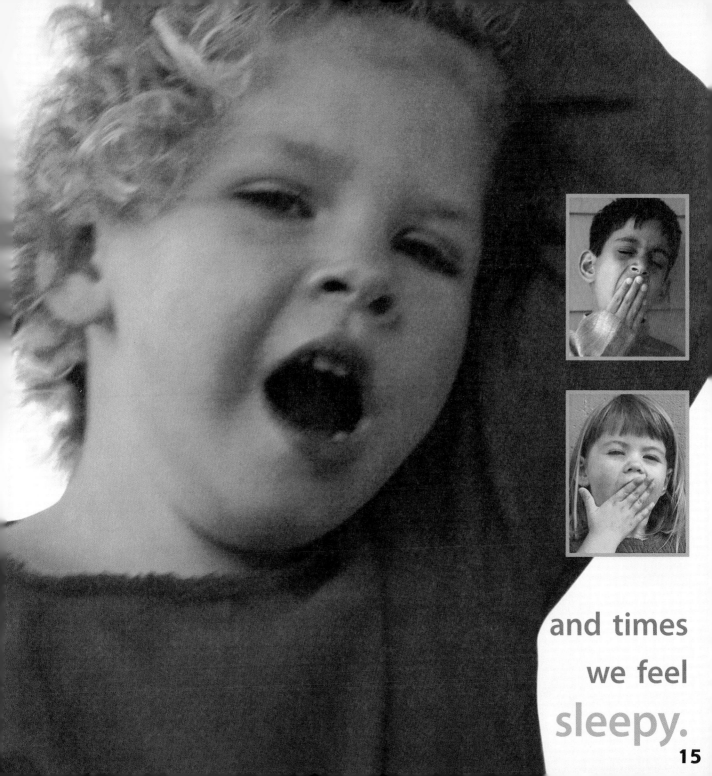

and times
we feel
sleepy.

At different
times we
feel
serious…

or **silly...**

curious…

or **confused.**

19

Everyone
has
lots of
feelings.

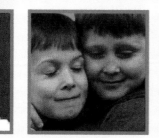

21

How about **you?**

id hyperactive wild sad vulnerable uneasy bored scared curious prett

nasty lonely doubtful terrific exhausted excited rowdy zealous embarrasse

frightened giggly awful weird terrible quarrelsome crazy happ

zany disgusted intimidated greedy lucky friendly itchy jealous delighted hu

sweet vain jittery kind gross furious enthusiastic perturbed loving eager funn

zestful mischievous jumpy uncertain dizzy clever miserabl

yucky nervous cool guilty nice anxious weak okay patient mad wacky excite

ashamed proud mixed-up pleased tired questionable ridiculous bashfu

energetic zonked rambunctious silly quiet overwhelme

negative sleepy glad insecure disappointed timid impatient joyful upse

sensitive vicious beautiful frustrated knowing irritable vibrant worried moody

generous exhilarated youthful active blue obnoxious calm afraid hyperactive

wild sad vulnerable uneasy bored scared pretty nasty lonely doubtful

terrific exhausted excited rowdy zealous embarrassed frightened brave

awful weird terrible quarrelsome crazy stubborn happy zany disgusted

intimidated greedy lucky friendly itchy jealous delighted hurt sweet vain

jittery kind gross furious enthusiastic perturbed loving funny zestful

mischievous jumpy keen uncertain dizzy clever miserable naughty yucky

nervous cool guilty nice anxious weak okay patient mad wacky excited ashamed